THE
GREATEST
LOVE

SEEKING & FINDING WISDOM

IRIS FERBER

DEDICATION

To the great memory of my parents,
who worked extremely hard
to overcome their many struggles.

And to my beloved children and grandchildren,
who teach and inspire me daily.

CONTENTS

Part I: The Greatest Love

Part II: Memories & Experiences

Part III: Where Am I Going?

PART I
THE GREATEST LOVE

GOD'S LOVE

There is no greater love or security than to know, accept, and receive the Love of God by faith. For underneath are the everlasting arms. The arms that will not let go. The love that will not walk away or change. The kind of love that we discover is the greatest the more we surrender to it.

This love is satisfying because we were created for it. The love of God is perfect love. It pushes out all fear. It is not something to be explained; it must be tasted.

STRENGTH AND BALANCE

Psalm 27: *God is the strength and center of my life.*

You may or may not feel like you really know God yet. At first for me, God was an idea, a passing thought... something that people talked about once in a blue moon.

I would hear about God at church when I was a child, but there was no introduction to a personal relationship. God was a distant idea, lovely but I couldn't really grasp it. Far away.

My paternal grandmother seemed "different," like she really believed in God. She was rather devoted to God but not obsessed with the idea. God was more like a beautiful fragrance that was woven into her life. She always seemed anchored, peaceful, centered, not easily moved by the surrounding drama of others. She was steady, strong, and balanced at eighty-five years of age. I decided when I was five that I wanted to be like her.

SEEK AND YOU WILL FIND

It happened for me when I was twenty-eight years old. Strangely, I came to "know the Lord" much like I would meet any person—through a series of events and experiences. An introduction, an encounter.

I was certainly in need of a change, a more meaningful life, but I didn't really believe God existed, so He had to prepare me through experiences. I think I was just existing, questioning whether this could be "all there is to life." But innately I sensed a knowing that there had to be more than what money could buy.

One day while sitting on my back porch with my two little boys, I noticed the neighbor's cleaning lady, Sharon, pull into the driveway on her scooter like she always did on Tuesdays and Thursdays. Sometimes her beautiful twelve-year-old daughter would ride on the back.

What really stood out to me was that Sharon was dependable, always friendly and joyful. I felt both curious and annoyed at the same time. What on earth could she be so happy about?

THIS BOOK

Well, one day I decided to ask her... Brooklyn style. We exchanged hellos as usual and then I asked Sharon what would become one of the most pivotal questions of my life:

> "What is with you anyway?
> Why are you always so happy?"

She said, "Oh, nothing. I just know Jesus and I read my bible."

I had grown up in a nice Jewish neighborhood. I read a lot of books about eastern religions and had even practiced some Buddhist chanting, yoga, Zen... but I had never read a bible or even been introduced to it in Catholic church as a spiritually curious child. Much less did I "know" Jesus. What was that?

I asked her, "Can you bring that bible to my house?" She replied, "Sure, I can come by tonight at 5:00." And she did... and on that day, my entire life changed.

I noticed something extraordinarily different about this book. The words seemed to have life. I know it sounds so weird but I have no other way to explain what happened.

I asked her, "What else do you do?" She said, "Oh, I go to church on Sundays." I asked if she would take me to her church.

I had already visited other religious temples. I was in a great space called *dissatisfied*. I was sort of sure that I needed something more, but I just didn't know what that was.

Well, she picked me up on Sunday morning just like she said. I can't remember the sermon to save my life. But what I will never forget is a song they played... a hymn... "Just As I Am." I went up to the altar and gave my life to Christ at this junction of what I now know to be the Holy Spirit moving upon me in a very real way.

I am not a person who cries easily. But I remember becoming emotional for a couple of minutes, and after accepting Jesus as Lord, never *ever* being the same again.

Decades of my questions seemed to vanish in what seemed like an instant as I realized and acknowledged this was the truth I had been seeking for a long time.

NO WORRIES

Ephesians 3:20: *He will give you abundantly above what you could ever ask or think.*

I never worry about running out of creative ideas, projects, doings, energy, provisions, or ways of helping or being generous to others. It just keeps on coming.

The more I utilize things, the more they multiply, but not in an obtrusive way. God's hand is so gentle and kind, he is so knowing and attentive to our needs, if we but genuinely, humbly look up and truly trust... here comes our help!

HOLY SPIRIT

Joel 2:28-29: *"It will come about after this that I will pour out my Spirit on all mankind; And your sons and daughters will prophesy, your old men will dream dreams, your young men will see visions. Even on the male and female servants I will pour out my Spirit in those days." (NASB)*

Jesus said he had to leave so that the Holy Spirit could come, so that we would not be alone, and that we would be comforted. The Holy Spirit is a comforter, friend, healer, revealer, and teacher of all truth. A present help in time of need.

Where the spirit of the Lord is... there is liberty. True freedom.

Are you kidding me? Welcome, Holy Spirit!

PRAY

I have been praying since I was a very little girl. I used to pray that I could have the scent and skin type my grandmother had. She wore no perfume or makeup. She had beautiful smooth brown skin and long silver hair. I wanted to be like her. She was a native Taino Indian from Puerto Rico. A sweet country girl.

I watched her faithfully pray her rosary three times a day. A real believer, Abuelita is still the most peaceful sweet-spirited, helpful, orderly, and soft-spoken woman I have ever known. Although she experienced much sorrow in her life, she had an undeniable internal peace, joy, and gentleness about her. A dependable steadfastness.

Now I know what was so different about Abuelita Maria. She had *something more*, and I know this because now I trust God myself, after having walked through many trials. "He has raised me too, on the winds of adversity."

PRAYER IS A BLESSING

Prayer blesses your life and prayer gives hope to those who are watching you and those whom you pray for. It is a rather simple discipline that provides more than we could ever think or imagine.

Just watching my grandmother and how peaceful she was, how gentle and orderly, forever enlightened and inspired me.

Prayer is an ongoing conversation with our loving creator. It is like any other communicative relationship. My granddaughter is three and always says, "We need communication, Grandma!" which is something she learned from a book I gave her on her birthday.

Prayer is a heavenly conversation. Don't worry about what other people think or say. Just remember to pray, ask, trust, believe, and seek God, and doors shall be opened to you.

SURPRISED ABOUT
PRAYERS THAT ARE ANSWERED

I used to go prayer-jogging with my great companion, Smokey dog. I prayed about whatever was on my mind.

Early every morning we'd pass a well-known biker bar one block away from our house. I would often pray that the bar would "close down because it was known for brawls and drug dealing and all that goes with that lifestyle."

My little prayer continued for a couple of years, and nothing seemed to happen. But when I pray, I also believe God will answer. Without that faith, it is impossible to please God.

BUT HE HEARS MY CRY

During our jog early one morning, I found a twenty-dollar bill on the road near the curb in front of the biker bar. The area was desolate then, even though it was loud and rowdy at night. I couldn't help but ask, "God, you are paying me, aren't you? Thank you!" It felt like the sweetest heavenly nod to me, as if to say, "Iris, I like that you care about your community."

What some people call "crazy," I call faith! When you practice faith, it grows. Kind of funny how we co-create our relationship with God.

It was springtime and business was booming at night at the bar. They built a beautiful, well-lit deck in the backyard with great loud speakers. The music didn't bother me much (because I love music), but I had three young children, so I was vigilant about the activity.

One night a really drunk man came relentlessly pounding on our door. It was close to 3:00 AM. Our whole family was awakened. It was pretty scary and all he kept repeating was, "It's me, Chip," as if we should know him. Apparently Chip, in his drunken stupor, thought he was somewhere else. Wow!

Things sometimes get worse before they get better. I continued my morning jogs and prayers, then lo and behold, the bar added a new feature—"topless dancers" on Thursday nights. Suddenly, our quiet little neighborhood, just a block away from our beautiful children's playground, was filled with trucks once a week. Needless to say, I was furious and in disbelief! But they were only interested in making money, and they were doing a great job at it. I had to change my game plan.

It became an urgent matter to me. It didn't matter if no one else was paying attention. I saw it as my assignment. I began to pray that God would simply have this building demolished. I prayed pretty consistently and with great fervor. I'm sure anyone else would think I was crazy, but I was passionate about my family and my community. Mostly I was passionate about my relationship with God. After all, if He wasn't going to answer, why was I praying?

One day to my amazement, Smokey and I went for our jog and there were demolition trucks tearing down the historical bar that had been there for decades.

Yes, that's exactly how it happened. A week or so later, The Old Wheel Inn was totally demolished. I asked neighborhood folks, "What happened?" They said the bar was purchased by a large manufacturing plant so they could *demolish* it (yes, demolish it) in order to build a much-needed employee parking lot!

Now, some folks might say that was a coincidence, because they have difficulty mustering up any faith at all, but I believe it was a miracle—and that's all that matters to me.

Sometimes folks tell me I have a special gift of faith and sometimes I believe it. But in this instance when God answered me so powerfully, I was totally humbled and surprised.

THE POWER OF JOY!

Nehemiah 8:10: The Joy of the Lord is your strength. (NIV)

Joy is different than *happiness*. Joy makes people smile and is contagious. Joy is an internal gift of God that shines from the inside out.

It may be without explanation, like "too good to be true." Joy transcends happiness, which can come and go. Joy may be something you either have and experience or you do not really know. Like the natural beauty of a river or an ocean or an extravagant flower garden, we can only *try* to explain that kind of overwhelming greatness.

What I do know is that joy is surely a power, a strength to endure, to run the race. I imagine if I lived without joy for too long, I would be somewhat hopeless and without great motivation. But joy basically empowers my life... brightens it up, helps me see more clearly. It removes the cobwebs and clouds and shows me the sunny side of the street.

Maybe the strength is in my willingness to count my blessings and dwell on them.

REALLY AWARE
AND REALLY CHANGED

Galatians 5:22-23: But the fruit of the Spirit is love, joy, peace, patience, endurance, kindness, goodness, faithfulness, gentleness, self-control; against such things there is no law. (NIV)

There is a grand phenomenon that occurs when a person is authentic and steadfast in their close walk with God. They become more like Him, and at times an oracle. It is a relationship by choice, like any other.

But I do know that when a person maintains a healthy relationship with God, seeking knowledge of Him through worship, prayers, reading, and obedience, a transformation takes place. A daily transformation into an instrument of love, joy, peace, patience, endurance, kindness, goodness, faithfulness, gentleness, and self-control.

That is the fruit of His Spirit.

And when the Spirit speaks, our hearts are undeniably moved. We know that we have been in the presence of God, because we are changed!

PEACE THAT
PASSES UNDERSTANDING

This peace that becomes available to us is a deep inner-peace. Unlike any that the world gives, it's good that we can't even comprehend it. It is a protective and providing peace. We don't know how it is possible to have an enduring peace in this challenging world that is often filled with demands, hurry, work, chaos, lies, and pain, but God knows and gives it freely to His children who believe.

This peace that we attain from God cannot be taught or found in people, places, or things. It's a peace that guides and heals and gives us great reason to have hope. A peace that shows us and helps us how to really appreciate that *life is good!*

Let go… let God. Seek after peace and you will find it.

Shalom.

PUT YOU IN A BOX

Folks try to put you in a box, so that you're easier to label and control. Freedom to be yourself is a vital thing. "But remember, you are fearfully and wonderfully made." You are not a toy, a pair of shoes to use, or a box of chocolates to enjoy and discard. You are precious and powerful.

One secret is that people can *never* put you in a box unless you let them. I love the martial arts concept of simply moving out of harm's way... it's so peaceful and so wise. Choose your battles, because most of them can be avoided by moving out of the way.

And be very careful with your life. People didn't give it to you. He whom the Son sets free is free indeed. *Do not return* to the bondage of men! Hang out with people who make you feel glad and let you be free!

LOVE YOURSELF

"You shall love the Lord your God with all your heart and with all your soul and with all your strength" (Luke 10:27). This is the great and first commandment. The second is that you *love your neighbor as yourself.* On these two commandments depend all the Law and the Prophets.

Wow! Number one, I am commanded to love the Lord my God with all of me.

Second, I will love my neighbor "as" I love myself. So, to me, that means if I love myself abundantly well, I am pretty much set up to love others that same way. But if I'm not loving others as well as I love myself, then I should get to loving God and myself more by spending quality time soaking in God's presence, which changes me for the better.

This happens at home meditating on a special Psalm or inspiring song, or by attending worship services wholeheartedly, or by serving wherever it is that I am called and equipped to serve.

PRAY FOR YOUR CITY

Pray firstly for the peace of Jerusalem. Why? Because it's a commandment that promises things will go well with you if you walk in love towards Jerusalem. This takes faith.

Pray for your own city, your own home, and your own family. Faith works by love. Prayer is a very powerful act of love. It's also a good way to release negative emotions and return to the balance of expressing thanks for our many blessings.

Prayer helps me see more clearly because I am no longer relying only on myself or feeling overwhelmed by the burdens that I can't successfully carry, because I was never meant to. I don't necessarily get to understand it, but I get to obey and be blessed.

EVERYONE HATES 'FESSING UP

James 5:16: Therefore, confess your sins to one another and pray for one another, that you may be healed. The prayer of a righteous person has great power as it is working. (ESV)

Humility is tough. But remember, we all fail, we all miss the mark, we all commit errors we know are wrong—which is what sin is.

There is a way that seems right to us that leads to darkness and even death. As soon as we become aware that we have done wrong, the best thing to do is confess it to God and to a trusted friend. This helps you clean up your act from the inside out. Confessing our wrongdoings is important to our wellbeing. We can make a list every day or once in a while and be truly sorry for our actions.

BEAUTY

Beauty is a lot of things, and a lot of things are beautiful. There are many songs and books and movies that are all about beauty. My mother told me, "Keep your eyes on the beautiful things, Iris."

Nature is most beautiful, yet beauty is in the eye of the beholder. You may notice beauty that I missed, because you were able and willing to pay more attention or focus. Anything that is beautiful is worth taking care of because it brings joy.

My granddaughter Izzy stopped me from stepping on a fly in her kitchen one day. "Grandma," she said, "how would you like it if a big giant came and stepped on us?" *Wow*, I thought. She said, "Let's take it outside, or better yet, let's let it fly outside."

You see, I didn't take time to think about the fly. It was just annoying me and I wanted it out of the house. But Izzy took time to think about that fly, and well, thoughtful people probably get to see more treasures, because they take the time to do so.

You are beautiful.

YOU HAVE
MORE THAN YOU THINK

Well, we woke up this morning and can read this page. Thank you.

Breathing, thank you.

If you have a roof over your head and shoes to wear, just be thankful.

I can move, help myself, pray, feed myself, help others, I am writing right now... So grateful!

Are you creative? Do you enjoy your world and are you good to it? Thank you.

I have awareness of the abundance of things that I am given on a daily basis. Thankful.

Obedience equals abundant blessings. My eyes can see, my ears can hear, my heart beats. With my voice, I can sing and praise.

LETTING IT GO

But where to? Sometimes people, places, or things can really irritate us. It almost seems that the more we care, the more they can distract and hurt.

I suppose these people, places, and things are not going according to our plans—sometimes by accident, sometimes on purpose. When this happens, every time I become aware of it, I try to practice "letting it go" as quickly as possible. When the problem seems stronger than my ability to let it go, then I must not only put it into God's hands, but I must also learn to leave it there and not take it back. This takes discipline and practice.

Yes, it gets harder before it gets easier. It takes practice and experience. Often I need to distance myself from a toxic situation in order to get a clearer picture of "my part" and what is going on here on a deeper level. I love the freedom that finally letting go brings.

As much as I hate to admit it, I am a problem solver who does not enjoy defeat. Letting go feels like failure, but every time I try *one more time*—ha-ha, it never works—that's how I finally learn to LET IT GO! Ugh!

"FEAR NOT, FOR I AM WITH YOU"

Sometimes "fear is a liar."

I recently heard a song with this title. But I thought, *Fear doesn't always lie. Sometimes it is our friend.* Like when it helps us not get burned or to hurry away from areas we perceive are dangerous. Fear sometimes even motivates people to flee from corruption, due to uncomfortable internal feelings about people, places, or things. That kind of fear is what I would call a good indicator of a true and present danger.

What about the other kind of fear?

False Evidence Appearing Real

There is a fear that subtly infiltrates our thoughts, that stubbornly takes up residence in our minds... and then quietly fuels and controls our feelings and eventually our behavior. That kind of fear must be arrested, because it can be all-consuming when permitted to run wild.

This fear can be paralyzing. It's not a smart warning to flee potential danger. It's invisible yet a powerful emotion. It can hold us captive if we don't catch it and deal with it. But how?

First, by noticing it. Admitting that it's odd and acting upon what we know is *truth*, is the antidote. Often this fear or anxiety ironically points to something that can be readily fixed if only it is seen, acknowledged, confronted, and disowned. Sometimes it's a controlling relationship issue. Just like the more positive fear, it demands that *action be taken*.

Again, it is usually a pointer or an indicator... perhaps a symptom of my own mistakes. This I can change; I have been given the power to change it. To take it captive, and ultimately rule over it.

I don't exactly know why fear is so prevalent these days. Maybe because of increased deception. I think awareness is key though. And my ultimate solution is "to not only be a hearer of God's word, but to be a doer of it." I must take action. Therein lies the blessing.

FASTING

I once fasted for eight days, only drinking water and when I felt hungry, I ate watermelon or a few pretzels. Fasting made me feel physically peaceful and more spiritually aware, clearer and calmer emotionally, less distracted by others' seemingly insignificant behaviors. Ironically, I rarely felt hungry.

I would say "peace" was the reward for fasting.

More recently, I spent twenty-one days on a much different fast. I ate no meat, almost no sugar, no sodas, and no breads... but did eat veggies, fruits, and whole grain rice. Again, there was a feeling of physical cravings being weakened, a sweet clarity, a pureness of speech because I was using fewer words, and I was made more aware of their meaning.

I'm smiling right now at just the thought that I did it.

I must do it again!

HELPING SOMEONE ELSE

Hebrews 6:10: *God is not unjust; he will not forget your work and the love you have shown him as you have helped his people and continue to help them. (NIV)*

Just about every day we come across an opportunity to help someone, to just be kind. Some days, more than once... helping a baby who has fallen to get up again... helping a parent carry a heavy load... giving someone a gift... doing a chore without being asked, or better yet, secretly.

We can spontaneous give a kiss on the cheek or a great big bear hug. We can really listen to someone who is lonely. We can bring a bit of peace to someone who is worried. We can speak an encouraging word. We can tend our garden plants and flowers, feed the birds, play with the kitty.

My all-time favorite help is *a smile.* A smile speaks every language and takes less effort than a frown. Think about it... then smile more often on purpose. You'll automatically become happier and more helpful also.

WISDOM

Proverbs 4:6-7: *Do not forsake wisdom, and she will protect you; love her, and she will watch over you. Wisdom is supreme; therefore, get wisdom. Though it cost all you have, get understanding. (ESV)*

After time passes, you tend to see the same situation in a different light because, along the way, you have gathered some wisdom. You can see the rewards and consequences of your actions. You've learned forgiveness, understanding, compassion, and patience because now you have experience and God-given wisdom in your toolbox.

Perhaps you used to just react to things, but now you know you have survived other tough circumstances, and overcome many fears. Now you are more settled, and more confident about who you are and what you can accomplish. You know you are much stronger than you thought yourself capable of being, and you are thriving when you thought you might not even make it through.

Wisdom is the principal benefit. Seek and find it, because it changes everything. Watch and learn from those who have walked this path before you.

DENIAL,
OR "IT'S MY BAD"

Ephesians 31-32: Let all bitterness and wrath and anger and clamor and slander be put away from you, along with all malice. Be kind to one another, tenderhearted, forgiving one another, as God in Christ forgave you. (ESV)

It happens to everybody, especially when stress is involved. We are subconsciously blocked from seeing our own issues. This can be a survival mechanism, but it can backfire. We can deny truth, but there is a price to be paid for not checking in with our true selves.

The problem with this habit of denying our issues is that they show up in our behavior—like they speak for us! Or even worse, they show up in our physical and mental health.

Other people clearly see, hear, and feel our issues manifesting, while we remain blind to them. And boom, just like that, now we've got even more problems to deal with.

Or… we can meditate, pray, and choose to gently, humbly, and fearlessly check ourselves by letting go of toxic negativity. By owning what is truly ours and letting go of what we cannot control. We can ask for forgiveness and strength to do better.

And boom, life gets a little lighter and a little sweeter, just like that!

To err… is human.

SPIRITUAL HUNGER

Psalm 143:6: I stretch out my hands to You; my soul longs for You, as a parched land. Selah. (NKJV)

We hunger and thirst for spiritual food. Our souls need to be fed and cared for. Nothing pleases God more than when one of us comes to the end of our own egotistical ideas and surrenders to His loving kindness.

It's not that life is easy as pie now. It's that you know your father loves and takes care of you... no matter what happens. Like the old song, "He's Got the Whole World in His Hands," as sung by Mahalia Jackson.

I learned this through living with an addict, being co-dependent, being a mother, and having family that could not really help me much.

Today I continue to learn and see God's hand fill and provide me with a peace that I may never understand, with a joy that is rather inexplicable. You either experience it or you don't. You either seek Him and believe or you don't. You're either hungry and thirsty or you're not. I am so thankful for spiritual hunger and the bread of life! Every word that proceeds out of the mouth of God, that is the bread of life.

LOVING YOURSELF

Proverbs 19:8: *To acquire wisdom is to love yourself; people who cherish understanding will prosper. (NLT)*

Being intelligent is a great gift. Learning to use our intelligence is what acquiring wisdom promises. We are hardwired to survive. So much can happen during a lifetime—good, bad and ugly. But wisdom gives us tools beyond simple survival. It teaches us how to soar above situations, prosper, give, love others, and keep ourselves safe from much harm.

Wisdom teaches how to be humble, pleasant, and laugh and cry. We learn that it's not just okay to be good to ourselves, caring for ourselves, body, soul and spirit, but that it is vital to becoming a better person.

Sometimes being good to yourself means just going to bed early or eating a bowl of cherries. Sometimes it's buying a new outfit or going for a walk in the park, planning a vacation or playing a game. Being with likeminded people is good for us. When we reasonably give ourselves what we need and enjoy, we feel happier. And when we are happier, we are more able to be kind and pleasant to others.

Don't Compare
Yourself to Others

We were wonderfully and uniquely made. Just look at any new infant.

Being yourself is a key factor in achieving contentment. After all, if you don't know who you are, how will anyone else really get to know you? How will you identify your true gifts and talents, your likes and dislikes?

If I should decide to compare myself to others, who would that be? After all, everyone else is taken!

Instead, I have decided to be my best self, every moment that I can. I am never perfect at it. I can be better at this game of life tomorrow. I can forgive myself for mistakes like I would forgive someone else. I am human, after all. God loves me and you!

FEELING PRESSURED

Go to the Father of Lights.

Deadlines, bills, fitness, school, planning, relationships, appointments and disappointments, health concerns, even our deepest desires and dreams coming to fruition can exhaust us...

The good, the bad, and the ugly often cause stress and pressure. The doggone news... damned if you listen to it and uninformed if you don't. How do we deal with it all before it overpowers us?

By noticing the pressure when it's rising and choosing to *lay our burdens down*. Life is too overwhelming some days for even the best of us.

Bring all of it to the altar and ask for help. Relinquish the tug of war for control.

Unto you, Father of Lights, with whom there is no variableness, neither shadow of turning we bring our cares, for you surely care for us.

PEACE

Peace is a vital human need, all-encompassing in its reach, more important than riches or talent alone. For after all, what good are riches and talent when we don't have peace?

I carefully pay attention to and guard my inner peace. To me, peace is the starting point of each day and the quiet rest of each night. Without it, I am too insecure to truly function well enough to do my daily activities with a spirit of excellence and joy.

During the 1960s and '70s, young people were so sure they knew what peace was. But most of what they discovered was a temporary external form of relaxation, brought on by comradery, music, physical love, sensory pleasure, and yes, substance abuse.

Lasting peace is not about colorful clothing, long hair, or amazing incense. It's definitely not about kindly flashing two V-shaped fingers at passersby. That's nice but it's not peace. Wearing flowers in your hair or getting tattoos and having a couple of drinks are temporary fixes at best. It just doesn't last. And when we must repeat these rituals, we can become addicted to them, which in turn takes away even the bit of peace we acquired.

Don't get me wrong. Purposely being relaxed, kind, creative, energetic, celebratory, loving, and enjoying nature and friendships are great things. But true consistent inner peace that surpasses understanding is a "knowing" that you don't have to do anything to maintain. Only God can give that gift. And I suppose He reserves the right to let us seek it in any other place, but only find it in Him!

When I began seeking the true meaning of life, I realized there must be more... and in continually seeking, eventually I met peace.

CONSIDER THE BLESSING

Whenever I lose my way, God, I am reminded to examine all of my blessings. It's overwhelming to try to count them. Even when I try, I am unable to recollect the countless times you've saved and blessed me. I so desire to appreciate your unstoppable goodness, I really do. Yet, amazingly once again I need your help! It's mind-boggling that even counting our blessings causes them to multiply. I cannot understand you but I love you and I know that you love me. I stand in awe of how great it is to be your child.

You were always there, and one day when you opened my eyes, I was able to see and accept your truth into my heart and mind. You only needed a tiny humble opening and a mustard seed of faith and you saved me from the mud.

How can I say thanks?

My Trust Is in You

You open and shut doors that no person has access to. You restored me when I was just a torn and tattered mistreated but beautiful tapestry who desperately needed healing. You gave me beauty for ashes. What manner of love is this?

Dear Lord, please teach me to count the ways, to review your amazing blessings, and to remember your promises, for you do not change!

INTERDEPENDENT

I became a very dependent, trusting, and overly responsible person, following a season of *wild* independence and a bit of irresponsibility. I finally found the middle ground (balance) after testing these extremes. Maybe that happens to kids who grow up not having people to trust.

At least that's the way it happened with me. I rather painstakingly unearthed interdependence as my favorite choice, having tested some wild, scary, and quite unhealthy paths in my journey. I found out that God loved me and was always able and willing to help me, if I would but surrender. I never knew that before. If someone doesn't teach you, it's hard to know.

So when I became a parent, I taught my children all that I could so they would not be quite as lost as I had been. Even though *wild* can be fun, my soul was still lost. I craved stability. Stability is healthy.

***John 3 1:2**: Dear friend, I pray that you may enjoy good health and that all may go well with you, even as your soul is getting along well. (NIV)*

GET TOGETHER

> **1 Thessalonians 5:11**: *Therefore encourage one another and build one another up, just as you are doing. (ESV)*

Dear Iris, get together with beneficial family and friends as often as you can. Don't be afraid to have people over. Yes, it means you have to tidy up and get food and cook or buy takeout or just make coffee. But it is well worth it. You will never know how much you can enjoy and learn from others unless you get together more often.

People encourage and build each other up in a loving way—chats, smiling, laughter. Socializing is very healthy. Having different types of friends helps keep life colorful and interesting. You may have some neighborhood friends, work friends, school friends, church friends, pool club friends... you get the drift.

Some love deep conversations while other like to go on wild adventures. Some family make great friends because they understand your history. Everyone has gifts, and when we get together and share, we all end up richer in happiness. Go ahead... why not? Kick it up a notch!

SOME THINGS ARE NOT
EASY TO FORGET

John 14:26: *But the Helper, the Holy Spirit, whom the Father will send in my name, he will teach you all things, and bring to your remembrance all that I said to you. (ESV)*

Believe it or not, I imagine there is a good reason some things are not easily forgotten. Although at times I struggle with short-term recall, others have memories of steel. Our brains are meant to help us "survive." I believe this is why certain people, places, or events are either remembered as either pleasant or dangerous.

When someone's actions hurt us deeply, it is a challenging process to forgive and forget. It is wise to forgive so that we can lightly move on in our journey with less baggage. It is just as smart to remember not to travel down that same road, unless you like pain.

Yes, we can have peace between us, as we are called to have peace with everyone, if at all possible. We can even love people but choose not to get so close that they can harm us again and again.

I highly recommend "learning from mistakes, honoring God's still small voice, acknowledging our own thoughts and feelings," and making small changes. This is both for our own good and for the good of others. Struggle and strife are not wise choices.

Love isn't that difficult. It just takes two to tango.

PART II:
MEMORIES &
EXPERIENCES

MEMORIES

Luke 2:19: *But Mary treasured up all these things, pondering them in her heart. (NIV)*

Great memories of wonderful people that I have been privileged to know return to encourage my soul... to give me hope, that love does exist, that people can be kind and generous... to remind me that the seemingly impossible, extremely beautiful, kind, loving, adventurous, and most of all highly creative moments that surpass my imagination or desire can and will happen. Those are really miracles.

We have memories of survival as well as rich enjoyment and beauty, memories of ease or of very hard work, memories of arrivals and departures, of attachments and of letting go.

I am so thankful for memories that inspire and guide me. Had I not experienced so much awe and wonder, my fresh vision would not be as vivid. I treasure memories, as even trauma teaches us great lessons. An elderly woman once told me: "We never forget the good people!" These words warm my heart.

EARLIEST MEMORIES

I vaguely remember wearing a hand-knit royal blue and white sweater that my mama said she knit "while she was expecting me."

Mom's love languages were gift-giving and random acts of kindness. I recall beach chairs that our family would sit on by the front of the house in the evenings after supper on Brighton 3rd Street in Brooklyn. They were older brick detached houses in a low middle-class neighborhood of mostly friendly working Jewish people and senior citizens. Many of them had escaped and survived World War II. They spoke broken English and Yiddish.

Our house was just one and a half blocks from the ocean. Mom told me she was actually at the beach with my aunt Nellie the day she went into labor with me in June. I certainly am a water baby and I often wonder if this is the reason why the ocean is my happy place.

As a child, we would go to the beach with Grandma Ava almost every weekend. She packed great bologna and cheese sandwiches with mayo for lunch. Our parents grew up in the Caribbean Islands, so the beach was like home to them. We had so much fun in the sand and in the water.

Ava always warned us to memorize the color of the towel hanging from the bars of our big beach umbrella in case we felt lost. But one day when I was just five, I wandered away and really did get lost. The beach was crowded and I looked and looked but couldn't find my family. I started crying. A stranger took me to the police house for lost children. I was so scared. It looked like a cage to me—a big screened-in room right under the boardwalk. My family came to get me but I can't remember that part. I was scared to death and glad at the same time.

I also remember when my father, who grew up on the U.S. commonwealth island of Puerto Rico, took me by the hand and asked if I wanted to go out to the "deep water." I immediately said, "Yes!" I really loved my father and trusted him, and I loved the water too.

He said, "Okay, you just hang on to my neck really tight. Don't let go and I'll take you for a ride." I eagerly agreed, and I cannot describe or forget just how exhilarating and exciting that deep-sea ride with my father was. It was definitely one of the most wonderful experiences of my life, and still is a powerful memory.

Curious and
Adventurous Still

I was just a girl who liked to learn and experience great adventures. I often fell and got hurt. I too often failed and cried. But I kept seeking and searching. I learned that pain was as good a teacher as any, and that great people and selfish people were educators. But most importantly, I learned that in this crazy chaotic scary world, God would hold my hand even more securely than my daddy once did.

I eventually realized that God was in my heart and would never leave or forsake me. He was not a person who would lie.

This sense of safety and protection makes one flourish. Birds and flowers don't worry about where their necessities come from. How much more important are we who are made in God's image?

In that infallible security system, I learned to trust and to share with others all that He had done for me.

A STRONG WOMAN

Nehemiah 8:10: *The joy of the Lord is your strength! (NIV)*

I have seen many strong women. My maternal grandmother was a strong matriarch, often disappointed or upset by how those around her were not measuring up. That was her way.

We all knew her generous yet somewhat rigid ways. She was adamant about having top brand names or nothing. This is one way to overlook our own insecurities and weakness, by demanding what is best.

She was a strong wonderful woman in her own way, but not a happy woman. A hard worker, a fighter— but not happy, not peaceful, not often joyful. She always had a complaint because many took her generosity and overly responsible nature for granted.

Be strong in the Lord and the power of his might. Trust and lean on Him and not upon your own understanding.

I watched my mother be a strong woman. A bit too kind and generous like her mother, yet fierce when people said things she didn't want to hear. I don't recall ever seeing her cry. Yell, lecture, complain, and give—yes, that she did do. She worked hard and she was very smart, ahead of the game, much like her mom. She learned quickly, but was unskilled in relationships—much like me. She liked some unhealthy escape routes and they didn't seem to work well in the long run.

Then there's me, myself, and I. I am a strong woman, too. I grew up watching, helping, and studying these strong hard-working women who overcame plenty of challenges and hurdles through determination. Yet by age twenty-eight I had tried doing life on my own strength for ten years. I had seen a lot of religious hypocrisy and was determined to find out what life was really about. It couldn't just be about money, sex, alcohol, drugs, and rock'n'roll like the culture dictated.

I understood rebellion and militancy but they did not sit well with me. For a time, I was like my mom, seeking out my own escape routes. From travel to religion to broken relationships... there had to be more to life than what I had seen. I really believe I became strong when I surrendered and acknowledged my weakness, my inability to find joy or peace on my own. My best prayer was probably "God, if you really do exist, please help me."

THE QUIET SUPERHERO CHILD

This child sees so much. His or her powers are great gifts from the Creator. Sensitive to others, often turning anger and frustration inward, they may try hard to save people, not realizing they need salvation, too.

All children are gifts from God. If only families could be a healthy safe haven for them. But everyone has their ancestral baggage, and sometimes we can't unpack the amazing things that God has put in our bags until someone who has vision and faith explains that. Then greatness is born and giftings are polished, because iron still sharpens iron.

May they always know how to love and be loved, how to help and not hurt others.

LEARNING FROM CHILDREN

When my daughter was four years old, I gave her an empty box in the toy room and asked her to put toys in it that she no longer played with or wanted. We would take the toys to a homeless shelter. A couple days later, I checked the box. It was full, and on the very top was her brand new expensive holiday Barbie doll. I tried to be discreet and diplomatic on how I would explain to her that I had reservations about giving that special doll away. So I said, "When I told you to put toys in here, I didn't exactly mean brand new ones that you haven't really played with that much." In no uncertain terms, and very kindly, she said to me, "Mommy, I thought about that. And I thought about what I would want if I was in the shelter. And I thought all those little girls probably get old dolls that are broken and have no hair... but I would really want a brand new, beautiful Barbie doll."

When my son was in middle school, he made a beautiful planter in ceramics class and painted around the bottom edge, he wrote in script, "To the most patient mom in the world." So there I learned that he did appreciate my efforts and love.

My oldest son loves the ocean as much as I do. He also taught me the power of quiet confidence and risk-taking. He's a man of few words, but when he speaks, an abundance of wisdom pours forth.

My point is, pay attention and learn from children. They are great teachers.

Belonging

Take a deep breath, and another. Realize that "I belong here." You were put here, sent here with a purpose. It's up to you to find your purpose, to deal with the baggage that others try to place on you. To unpack and develop the great gifts that God has placed in you to be responsible for.

It's not your job to copy other people or to give them so much power that they get to define who you are, how you think, or what you get to do.

You are here (smile) because you belong here. If someone has a problem with that (while you're being a good person) then that is their problem to solve.

Move in closer to what makes you happy and step a bit away from the rest, every day. Welcome to this wonderful world!

Listen to Louis Armstrong's "What a Wonderful World."

You Have More than You Think

Sometimes we forget how many blessings we are privy to, how much peace and joy we have been given. We forget how many wonderful people, places, and things have crossed our path, how many extravagant fragrances and natural wonders we have experienced. We tend to forget how many times we have heard the awe-inspiring sounds of the sea and the "I love you" spoken to us.

How many times have we gotten to carry a totally dependent tiny infant in our arms? How incredibly powerful that little bundle of joy was! How many times were we saved and delivered from great and terrible danger?

Let's remember the pitter-patter of rain on the roof and the cool breezes that come through our windows on a warm summer night. And most of all, let's remember the smiles of those precious souls we have come across—big wide vivacious beautiful smiles that we mirror right back without a thought.

Listen to Nat King Cole sing "Smile."

COURAGE

"True courage is choosing to face danger while afraid, and that kind of courage you have in plenty."

—From the Cowardly Lion in *The Wizard of Oz*

It's the ability to determine to do something that really frightens us. Some examples include the high dive, singing in public, jumping double-Dutch, being unprepared for an exam, feeling vulnerable in a relationship, facing a bully, being a victim, getting sick, experiencing childbirth or an unplanned pregnancy, or being homeless, abandoned, or penniless.

You get the picture because you have your own list. You already know!

Ask for courage and strength, and you shall receive. *The joy of the Lord is your strength!* Get lots of it and be very strong. Laugh often. Watch funny movies and enjoy comedians. It is healthy to laugh.

But I Need More Courage

Remember... anyone who has accomplished a daunting task has probably felt terrified. Courage confronts and helps us move forward in spite of fear, doing what we know we must do.

I once gave my son a symbolic token of this courage as a birthday gift to carry on his key chain. He had been a great baseball catcher for over a decade, full of heart and determination. As an adult when he was blessed to be facing big business promotions, I knew it had to be scary... so I asked him to look at the key chain. It said, "Jesse, it's just like Little League." He knew exactly what I meant and still does. I got one of the biggest smiles that I'd ever seen from him.

In life, we walk through so many things that we are naturally afraid of doing. We often forget that we have been building courage muscles since we were very young.

As toddlers, we were afraid to get up and walk after falling down so many times. It probably seemed easier and safer to crawl, or to hold on to people and things and just never let go. Letting go can be so scary, but it means trusting. It means freedom and accomplishment.

My friend, you and I were not created for fearful gripping and dependence but for true freedom, trust, and interdependence with our Creator. We will scrape our knees, and our feelings will sometimes get hurt, but we will heal, and in so doing we will be stronger and more courageous than before.

"I LOVE FACING MY FEARS," SAID NO ONE EVER

I love the Lord and how He is always present in my time of need. I have faced mountainous fears. I have lived through situations where I thought it highly possible that I could die.

There are times when we just can't back out. Those situations are meant for us to endure, to grow from, to learn and to develop great faith from saying, "With my God I climbed that mountain." Remind yourself, *I fought that disease. I overcame that accident that tried to kill me. I learned to deal with people who didn't have my best interest in mind.*

I am thankful for these lessons. Can't say I'd like to relive them, but I'm grateful for them.

PARENTS

My parents were as kind as they could be, and they did the best they could with what they had. In that way I am just like them. I can only give my children what I have, so I humbly hope my children will honor my efforts and my good deeds rather than dwell on my many mistakes. I must say it took me a long time after becoming a parent myself and moving through the good and not-so-good turns of life to begin to appreciate all that my parents did despite their shortcomings.

So, honor your parents in the best ways that you can. Think of the good they did for you—how you probably wouldn't be here without them and their many sacrifices. Think about the fact that God chose them to be your parents and they chose each other.

Nobody has perfect parents. Humans are all broken people in one way or another. Give honor where honor is due, and when in doubt, say a prayer and ask for help.

Be thankful, and it will go well with you.

ABUSE

There are people who have not truly developed the ability to care about the needs of others. They are not empathetic. This is not totally their own fault, so try not to remain upset about what you can't change.

The principal thing is that when you recognize it, set clear boundaries. Keep a safe distance. Get the help you need, and pray for yourself as well as for the person if you can.

Hurting people, hurt people. So, one of the most important things is to get help for your own healing so you can break these often-familial chains.

We all hurt each other once in a while. This is natural because we are all imperfect beings. Yet our close relationships should not consist of excessive pain or hurtful patterns of any kind. When we hurt others, we should be able to talk it over and fix the problem lovingly.

Sometimes people are too broken and insecure or immature and need to seek professional help. You cannot make someone else get help. But you can change the situation significantly by getting some help and changing your own life.

FATHER'S DAY

I can never explain how great my father was for me, or how much he still means to me three decades after his departing from this world. I can never count the good memories, and I haven't many painful memories about my dad.

I recall missing him terribly when my mom broke up with him and remarried. I was heartbroken but eventually we reunited. He was strong in many ways. Perfectly imperfect, but to me he was almost everything.

It was my father's kindness and steadiness that actually helped me to believe in and trust my perfect unfailing heavenly Father. It was my earthly father that I had worshipped as a little girl and so I knew what true worship was when I encountered the Heavenly King.

Exodus 20:12: *"Honor your father and your mother, that your days may be long in the land that the Lord your God is giving you." (ESV)*

IT'S NOT *HOW MUCH* I KNOW

When I was in school, I learned that the student with the highest number of correct answers or most knowledge was very often rewarded. Especially, if they were able to display the ability and desire to follow the class rules.

So, I got good grades in class and on annual tests. I was told what a wonderful reader or math problem solver I was and what grade level my answers scored. Now there were even more rewards to be had, like I was offered to skip seventh grade! Sounds great, right?

Well, I tried this special program which was called the SP program in New York City at the time. I felt smart at first. I mean, I was just a regular kid who got her work done so she could play outside with her friends. I had never really evaluated myself as smarter than anyone else, but I learned that just a few students were chosen for this program.

The only problem I faced after a couple of months in this classroom was that I have always been a very social person. Hmm... another thing I hadn't noticed about myself!

Anyway, I was miserable in SP class because *nobody* spoke to each other or passed notes. They didn't play ball in the schoolyard either, which was something that I loved. They weren't interested in pop songs, dances, or going out in groups for yummy deluxe hamburgers and French fries or pizza at lunchtime. All they did was study. I was like Eeyore, blue as could be. I may have scored well enough on the tests but I really didn't fit in. I felt unhappy.

I was only thirteen and had little real knowledge of who I was or what made me happy. My family was too busy trying to survive to pay much attention to these important details of a child's life.

"Knowledge is being aware of what you can know and do. Wisdom is knowing when not to do it."

"Knowledge helps you make a living. Wisdom helps you make a life."

I Don't Know That Much

Poetry Corner
Open up your mind.
Life is so seemingly simple,
yet so realistically deep.
For every event of an instant
there is a purpose and a reason,
but some seem to overlook for even
the length of a season
that God is in power
and that He ultimately decides
to protect, or divide, according to who
is on His side.

The scientist tells me this is not so...

"But the plants make carbon dioxide and fruit," I say. "We need that stuff to stay alive, to stay alive, you know."

What other reason can you give me for this obviously super-human perfection in every living thing?

What about the super ingenious phenomenon we call nature?

Why do the trees grow?

Why do humans have the brains to figure out scientific technology, if it wasn't first meant to be?

In our finite reality we are sometimes only important to ourselves.

To God, every one of us and everything that breathes, every living thing is important, for He provided perfection in all for all.

It is often our gift of free will that rebels and ruins the perfection.

And somehow the evolution of this unbridled free will may be victorious after all...

For it will cause us to self-destruct.

—Iris Vargas, circa 1984

A KNOWING

I know this is a gift. It's all a gift. Sometimes... often times... I see things coming. It is like a warning or an alert. Other times it's a feeling, or something I see in a dream or in a thought or even a quick vision. I always wonder, "Why me?" But the truth is, "Why not me?" It is often an ability to make a quick decision without any analyzing, which is not like me.

For example, the other day I went to the Dollar Store. While walking into the ladies room and realizing that I only had my small yellow wallet in hand and not my purse, I had this thought: *Oh, I better be careful not to lose my wallet.* Simple, right?

Oh no... I looked down and right before my eyes, what did I see? An old worn-out black wallet. Somebody must have thrown that out and bought a new one, then just left it on the floor. But no! I opened it up and it was full of every ID, credit card, grandchildren's pictures, cash and bank card.

Oddly enough, this woman had many of the same cards I have in my wallet. It was just strange. I asked around the store for someone who had the unusual first name on the ID. Nope, no one. I wouldn't leave the wallet with the cashier—too risky for a girl like me, so I drove down all these back winding roads to the address on the driver's license.

Finally, the lady was really happy... but the odd thing was she hadn't even realized she had left her wallet at the store where she works. I believe it was intuition that made me think *I should be careful not to lose my wallet* in that bathroom. It was a strange event at best, with a really happy ending.

Some people might have kept all the money or used the cards. I wouldn't be able to live with myself if I did that.

DISAPPOINTMENTS

Psalm 30:5: Weeping may endure through the night, but joy comes in the morning. (KJV)

Life is good, yet occasionally it is tainted with brief and upsetting disappointments. Even though we pretty much know that everything happens for a reason, often that reason does not become clear until later, when we are no longer right smack in the middle of the disillusionment and after the wound has started to heal.

Remember that we are always learning and that we probably won't repeat this mistake again if we have learned from it.

Don't lose confidence. Every human being makes mistakes and we all suffer disappointments. Things don't always unfold as we hoped or imagined. And they certainly don't always go our way.

"We must accept finite disappointment, but never lose hope." —Martin Luther King, Jr.

JEALOUSY

To the pure in heart all things are pure.

Jealousy isn't my thing, maybe because my mother warned me that it was not a good thing when I was still a child. Mom said, "We should always be happy for others when something good happens for them." She was really right about this one. It may seem too simple but it's true. When we identify and dismiss jealousy (as a habit), we have more peace of mind.

We leave more space to be thankful and focused on what we have rather than on what we don't have. And being thankful is a very big part of joyfulness.

Everyone gets a little jealous sometimes, but don't stay there. It's much healthier to be grateful.

LONG-LASTING FRIENDSHIPS

Proverbs 18:24: *A man of many companions may come to ruin, but there is a friend who sticks closer than a brother. (NIV)*

When a child grows up in a family that moves to many different places, it is challenging and almost impossible to develop long-lasting friendships. But we do have more choices when we grow up. We can choose the same chaos or more stability if we like, which I highly recommend.

We can choose to "bloom where we are planted," for a season that lasts as long as we like.

Then there is a greater chance of meeting and developing long-lasting friendships with just a few people. Even one will do. An amazing gift, a great opportunity that God gives us when we're not looking—a chance to build an extended family of friendship.

LOYALTY

I learned to be loyal to the underdog. I'm not sure when, but to this day it is the same. I may have been under five years old. I knew what it was like to watch and hear an out-of-control bully. I knew what it felt like to be bullied.

Once I knew what it felt like, from my point of view, it left me no choice.

This is a two-sided coin because sometimes I defend someone, only because I perceive they are the underdog. This is not such a bad thing. But I must be aware that people are able to recognize this pattern in me and sense that I have a soft touch... and take advantage of it. This I learned from my biker friend/neighbor Jim. "A real gentle tough guy."

LEARNING ABOUT REST

> **Matthew 11:28**: *Come to me, all you who are weary and burdened, and I will give you rest. Take my yoke upon you and learn from me, for I am gentle and humble in heart, and you will find rest for your souls. For my yoke is easy and my burden is light. (NIV)*

I grew up around some wonderful Jewish people in Brighton Beach in Brooklyn, New York. But I didn't know Orthodox Jewish people until I moved to Sea Gate. My landlady, aka Aunt Mimi, was Orthodox and so were many of my neighbors. I learned a lot by observing their traditions and lifestyle choices.

"Aunt Mimi" was kind yet quite quirky. We grew to really love each other. Yes, you can love someone who is very different and whose beliefs are not your own, and they can grow to love you. That is what I call a miracle if we want it. Some have eyes to see and others are stuck on rules. The law is a magnificent thing, but it is the *spirit* that brings life.

I learned about the Sabbath from Jewish people. On Fridays, the women prepared all things so that from sundown Friday to sundown Saturday, all was peaceful and rest was in order. No cooking, no working, and for the strictly Orthodox, no turning light switches on and off.

In order to keep the law, my neighbor once asked me a favor that sort of made me feel both honored and like chopped liver at the same time. She needed a light switch turned off... and well, I was a *shiksa* (a non-Jewish girl). I don't think she meant the sting. I think she just wanted to do the right thing.

The funny part was during the week, she loved listening to Men at Work while smoking cigarettes on the rear deck. She told me she and her hubby were "first cousins." Yet would she touch the light switch on Saturday? No way. That's religion for you. Although Jesus said, "true religion is visiting the prisoner and the fatherless." He was kind of against the other kind of religion, in a "don't mess with me" kind of way.

I learned the power of rest one day every single week like clockwork—slowing down, doing nothing, but being with family and going to worship. This was an awesome lesson I never forgot, and I still try to aim for it in spirit.

Rest equals reflection, renewal, and restoration, especially if our rest is based on a love of spending time with God and good people.

LEARNING WHAT LOVE IS

1 Corinthians 13:4-5: Love is patient, love is kind. It does not envy, it does not boast, it is not proud. It does not dishonor others, it is not self-seeking, it is not easily angered, it keeps no record of wrongs. (NIV)

I've seen these words save relationships. In my youth I was both over- and under-protected. My family did the best they could, like most families do. But due to various influences, I didn't get to fully understand men. I didn't get to spend enough time around my father and my uncles before my family sort of fell apart.

This created havoc in my youthful relationships. I was shy, and it took a lot of time for me to feel comfortable. Some people are happy to take advantage of one's weaknesses. Men are hunters by nature. Girls need to know how they operate in order to avoid the perpetual net, yet be close enough to get to know them.

I don't believe that men are creatures who enjoy settling down, at least not as much as most women do. So I think it takes a lot of intelligence, wisdom, and love to create a home with a man. When I love, I am undeniably vulnerable and I do not enjoy that place any more than you do. But when I am guarded, I remain pseudo-safely alone.

Men like fun women who play and laugh and eat and drink and are merry. Probably so they can eventually catch them off guard. That's just my general point of view. Men are great adventure leaders and need someone to enjoy the adventure with, even if it's watching a football game. Hopefully that's not the total experience. LOL.

We are the glorious light on earth that they love to enjoy, the ones who give joyous direction to the adventure, add laughter and affection to the game. I believe that we learn from one another, but perhaps women teach men more. While they are busy, driving or changing the channels or looking for food to eat, they learn how to live life more fully with a woman who loves herself, her God, and him. And that makes for a happier life.

Sometimes I work in New York. I saw a man from India in the Manhattan hotel elevator. He was carrying coffee to deliver. I made a comment about it to which he responded, "It's for my wife. Then life will be happier." I wholeheartedly believe that man was on to something. Women respond and return favors that men do, in ways that cannot even be measured. We were created with gifts to give and those gifts are ignited or inspired by love.

MIDWEEK MONSTERS, OR LESSONS I LEARNED FROM MY BEAUTIFULLY IMPERFECT EARTHLY FATHER

Sometimes this world makes me wonder. But for me, this is the bottom line:

We are so very loved that we have been given a free will. We are free to "choose good over evil," or vice versa, from out of His amazing fountain of generosity.

My earthly father would sometimes (in my view) act like a "cheapskate." He was an observant wise man of few words. Something I heard him say more than three times was: "Be nice, Iris. It doesn't cost you anything."

I admit that before knowing the true God, my father was definitely *it*. I *worshipped* him. After all, he was the wisest, greatest, most fun, kind person I had ever met. Even his discipline was thoughtful, creative, and effective... a man who knew his power, but didn't weild it.

Every one of us must choose. "Be nice," he would say when I was wavering like a good kid. Later in life it was intriguing to me that I never saw the word *nice* in the bible. I think he meant, "Be good, Iris. It doesn't cost you anything."

But that wasn't exactly true either... was it?

DISAPPOINTMENT

Sometimes I get really disappointed though it doesn't happen too often anymore (thank God). I suppose I've learned from past painful situations to not trust easily, to not invest too much too soon, and most importantly, to guard my heart with all diligence.

It would be ideal if we were taught everything we need to know before we ventured out into the world. Unfortunately, we leave home with only the tools we were provided. Then we learn. We fall, we get hurt, we trust, and we may be betrayed. We love and allow someone to break our heart.

Others have issues too... and perhaps have fewer skills than you were taught. My guess is the amount doesn't matter because we all get hurt and we all learn from disappointments. I hate that part, but it does happen. I am not immune to getting hurt. What I am privy to is being healed, learning, and trying over and over. Eventually, success will be so much sweeter and glorious than the disappointment of failure can ever be.

Love never fails. So, if it fails... it wasn't love.

Dear Iris, please try to remember that!

ON BEING VULNERABLE

Well, I hate the feeling of being vulnerable. You probably do, too. But without a risk, there is absolutely no return. How safe is too safe?

We have to take risks even though we're human and we really enjoy feeling safe and comfy. Get out of that comfort zone, and take a chance. The worst that could happen is the worst that could happen. But on the other hand, something great happens when you take a risk and when you feel vulnerable. Yes, vulnerable. You actually grow and end up stronger, no matter the outcome. 😊

So You Feel Very Tired

I received a surprising and humbling message that also made me very glad. Good or bad, if it's intense, it makes us tired.

On Saturday, I attended a previously scheduled intensive training on one of my favorite activities— singing. On Monday, I flew out to Houston. Both flights were delayed and packed. I was kind (I mean, clueless) and volunteered to check my luggage because the airline was running out of overhead space. I meant well, but the airline lost my luggage. I looked on the conveyer belt... no luggage... then spent an hour making a claim after I was already exhausted.

Oh, then the car rental company was out of vehicles, and I had to wait in a long line. I arrived in Houston so much later than planned. It was dark when I drove that six-lane freeway. Let's just say it was painfully exhausting.

When you're very tired and hungry, first pray, eat, drink, rest, and sleep well. Be grateful that He got you through it all and that you're alive. Tomorrow is another day. Rest peacefully and be restored. Hugs.

BEST FRIENDS

It takes a long time to know, and friendship takes a long time to grow. One day you may turn around and see the years flew by, but your friend is still on your side. You take each other soup or go down to the beach. You sit side by side in church or on a bus trip to D.C. You know one another so well and have family stories you share with each other.

A dance of closeness and space, you walk and never race. This person is a treasure in life who brings little stress or strife.

Be a friend and have a friend, and you're twice as strong as you thought.

Proverbs 18:24: *Remember, there is a friend that sticks closer than a brother.*

FAKE NEWS

Seek truth.

So, I get a text with a hysterical video attachment regarding my workplace. I'm grateful for the belly laughs that are so needed in this stressful world we live in. Then I sleep on it. I get a good night's sleep.

In the morning I text my friend back with a reality check.

> *"I think this is fake news, buddy, with a twist of reality woven into it. Approximately 20 percent of the time folks are uncaring, incompetent, rude, obnoxious, and/or ego-driven. But the truth is that nearly 80 percent of the time people are caring, intelligent, and truthful. My numbers may be off in either direction because I am human too, but I can clearly see and know what happens in my workplace."*

SATISFACTION

Matthew 5:6: *Blessed are those who hunger and thirst for righteousness, for they shall be satisfied. (ESV)*

When you're as old as I am, you remember the wonderful years of classic crazy rock'n'roll. It influenced and helped form the thought life of many young people who were either tired of the "establishment" or wanting to fit in, or who loved a good rhythmic beat. But for whatever the reason, a huge hit by the Rolling Stones shared, "I can't get no satisfaction." The lyrics were raunchy at best. But in 1965 in most music, sex seemed to be everything.

Not to take away from its vital beauty and importance, we humans can get things wrong when we listen only to compartmentalized popular news, songs, fears, and trends while ignoring the wisdom of the ages. We can also become unbalanced when we don't see how needy we were created to be. And so we teeter-totter, trying to find lasting *satisfaction* in so many ways. Yet I am not sure that we were created to find satisfaction in anything other than staying very close to our Creator. That's what I see from my point of view.

Philippians 4:11-13: Not that I speak from want, for I have learned to be content in whatever circumstances I am. I know how to get along with humble means, and I also know how to live in prosperity; in any and every circumstance I have learned the secret of being filled and going hungry, both of having abundance and suffering need. I can do all things through Him who strengthens me. (NASB)

INCLUSION

When I was young, my grown-ups used quite a few inappropriate words. Then again, they called people what they were, much like an umpire call strikes or fouls. They didn't think twice in my family; they just blurted things out.

Then little by little, people started using new words, making new rules, trying to fix everything they thought was wrong. Don't say "fat"; say "overweight." Don't say "spic," for crying out loud; say "Hispanic." Never say "retarded"; just say "intellectually challenged."

The only problem was they could never get it right because no one was happy with the new labels, so they kept making up newer ones. What started out as perhaps a nice gesture became an endless war, an endless list of demands and disappointments... because nobody could get it right, because nobody was happy enough with themselves.

The only right way to include everyone is to actually care and include them... and to be perfectly imperfect friends, neighbors, family, or coworkers. It sounded so simple.

FRIENDS

Over the years you will probably make many acquaintances during your life's adventures. A few will turn out to be warm friends that you can develop with, learn from, share fears with, cry with, and enjoy belly laughs with, but some people will turn out to be rather cold, shallow, selfish, and sometimes even heartless.

Give your attention to the people who are kind to you, even if there's just one or two of them. Grow those relationship seeds, first and foremost. Feed and water them with your own acts of kindness, service, affection, gifts, and affirming words.

The people we remember and love to spend time with most are usually warm, caring, loyal, and kind. These are the folks we feel comfortable with, and who, if need be, we can depend on without worry. They keep their promises whenever they can and they have our backs when we're in need. They communicate with us and we understand each other fairly well.

If they are humble and generous to us, it could be so easy to take them for granted. But if we want a really healthy friendship, we must pay attention, care, respect, and appreciate them. We keep a balance and that equilibrium maintains lifelong friendships. One cannot always be the giver or the non-stop taker; nobody wants to grow weary in well-doing. Just be present, because in order to have a friend you must be one.

Sometimes friendship reminds me of a see-saw. It's this scary give and take that makes it necessary for two active players to exert similar amounts of energy. It's the push and pull that makes it fun and exhilarating. It requires skill, practice, energy, and desire. It becomes loyalty, intention, peace, and joy in the midst of an often-chaotic world.

Sometimes humans disappoint each other, but when it comes to chosen friends, frustration and disappointment should be the exception and not the rule.

"A real friend loves at all times."

RESILIENCE

I once attended an unforgettable training. Neuro-scientists have determined that "it takes a village" is good in theory. But the fact is that if a child has one person who cares and provides for them, disciplines and guides them well throughout his or her formative years, then they can have great success in life, despite the odds.

I'm not an activist... or maybe I am in a different way. I try to be "that one person" as often as I can.

I learned that from my father first.

THE JOY OF WORK

"In your presence is fullness of joy." When I just acknowledge that the Lord loves me and truly believe it, there He is!

When I am kept busy at a task that needs to be done for the sake of my own peace—or that I finally choose to do because it brings me joy—then I really need to get into it. I may not be that good at first, because nobody is, but I get into exploring it more deeply and doing it with a spirit of excellence. Not perfection. I may even dislike the task, but shortly after deciding to start, I can get lost in it. Like singing, for instance. It can make me so nervous, but the more I prepare, practice, and acknowledge how it temporarily and ultimately makes me feel, the more I study and the more joyful it becomes. Not easy, not perfect... but joyful.

That joy may simply be in being helpful to another soul, or accomplishing some tedious tasks that were dreaded and procrastinated... like vacuuming. But Michael Jordan's "Just do it" is profoundly true., Lately, I've brought myself closer to "the doing" and further away from the "thinking about it." I feel better already. Doing something that I feel called and equipped to do? Now, that's the ticket!

THEY JUST WOULDN'T LISTEN

I don't know what they were thinking... be it obstinate, heedless, contrary, oblivious, stubborn, or ignorant, these folks just don't really hear and do what makes sense to others. Yet as much as you may love them, worry not. They too have rewards and consequences. My suggestion is to put their names on your loving prayer list and move on to something more productive for you or someone else.

These folks may actually change when they can no longer waste other people's words, time, or energy. Erase the expectation from your mind. Just let them be themselves. And you go ahead and mind your own business and work on being you!

RELATIVE DISAPPOINTMENTS
AND PAIN

Disappointments and pain are like the stinging part of knowing truth. I recently had a terrible time with wasps on my porch and deck. Apparently, I knew little about their retaliation methods... and I disturbed their nest. The sting from a wasp can be very painful.

Sometimes, we disturb people when we are in search of truth. So, what should we do? Just leave it alone? Or suffer days of pain, swelling, and incredible itch, hoping medication will help us get through? I suppose it's our choice.

I liken this retaliation to problems with insecure (and often deceitful) people. Face the issue, investigate it, then get rid of its venom. This is an important form of self-care and protection.

But oh, the sting! Yet a sting is temporary. It is not like having to live with lifelong dis-ease. It passes in just a few days, and knowing the truth sets us free.

Thank God for the revelation, for the pest control, and for wisdom, though the process is a painful one for a moment in time.

PART III:
WHERE AM
I GOING?

THIS IS THE DAY!

The first thing I say out loud in the morning is:

"This is the day that the Lord has made. I will rejoice and be glad in it!" (Psalm 118:24, NKJV*)*

I acknowledge that I am not in control of all things. God is. This teaches me to be thankful. My assignment is to rejoice and be glad in it. I encourage myself.

I can't explain how powerful of a starting point this creates for me. How I start a thing is usually how it goes. Gladness is a powerful word and a way of being that I learned so much about from a little book written by Christian D. Larsen called *Just be Glad.*

If we have even one choice (and we always do), it begins with how we think, and is reinforced by what we say most often. I live by this code as much as possible—not "perfectly." I fall seven times a day, but I keep getting up. I shake it off and keep going.

I try to catch stray thoughts and nip negativity in the bud, though I fail often. But this is the day! I get one day at a time. Worrying about yesterday, tomorrow, or things that I can't control is futile. Today is real. It's here and now, and I can work and play in it, but

I'm reminded that I did not create this day; it is a gift. A wonderful gift, like a fresh slab of clay to the sculptor.

Rejoice and be glad in it! To me it's like the good part of childhood, where you are joyful and play so much, have friends, learn, sing, and play ball or dance. Because of this core belief and action, when troubles show up, my mind is stronger, more relaxed, not full of worries!

I framed this affirmation and hung it right at my bedside, so I can remember it every morning. It's sort of like a basketball player getting into position to shoot a foul shot or swimmers positioning themselves to dive. Moments of preparation really count and they often predict how well things will go.

This is the day! 😊

JOY

Joy is an inside job.

Jesus said to first clean the inside of the cup. Maybe because I have such a tendency to look outside myself for happiness, I hope for a relationship being just the way I would like it to be, or a beautiful gift, a car, or a vacation that I can magically use without having to work hard at it. It could be the idea of a beautiful house in just the right location or even the greatest outfit or shoes... (I'm a shoe girl).

None of these things are wrong. Actually, they are all good, but their effects are temporal. As a matter of fact, shortly after I attain something, I begin to take it for granted (at least a little bit) and look to the next thing on my list to acquire.

Joy is different. Joy seems like a bank account inside of me that gets filled to overflowing by blessings that I am sharing with others, although I can pray and ask for them. Joy is a moment that seems like a lifetime, a rich blessing that I cannot contain, something or someone that makes me feel so humble, happy, and thankful that it leaves a mark and is sealed in my soul. Then it pours out to someone else. This too I do not control.

My maker is my best perfect joy-bringer. I will praise Him, for He alone is worthy. He knows what I need more than I do. It is past my understanding. I can just receive and be thankful and willing to share it because I realize that its source is without end.

Love and joy are fruits of the Holy Spirit—a sign that we have been in His presence.

HEALTH

3 John 1:2: My will is that you prosper and be in health even as your soul prospers.

Health is a given. I hear it in my spirit. It's about taking care of the great healthy body that carries me everywhere I go and is so good to me. It's about my very own soul's prosperity.

Yes, it's about my soul. Although, at times I drop the ball, I just am so inclined to pick it up again in thanksgiving for the great gift of this wonderful body that is so good to me.

Sometimes I totally take it for granted or mistreat it... but I know I must turn it around and do the right thing for myself.

I love to sing, dance, and swim. What do you love?

THIRST

"Hydrate," they say. "Your body is more than seventy-five percent water."

We can't exactly wrap our minds around that, yet we try to drink lots of water, because after all, who doesn't want to stay healthy? Plenty of water does wonders for the health of our bodies. But it's challenging for me to consistently drink as much as is so often recommended.

Maybe that is a sign for me. It's a great goal that most try to reach for. Yet over the years I've noticed that nutritionally, we can ignore all other needs when bombarded with one thing to focus on. So, I try to relax and find a balance. When I see myself about to fall to one side or the other of the seesaw of life, I can drink water.

Our emotional and spiritual needs are also in need of hydration, so let's remember that we are much more than the body we dwell in. Balance is key, and of course we cannot expect to do it all right all the time. It's too much. We have almost endless needs. So, let's aim to do the most important things well. I'm sure that will help us.

WALK IN LOVE

Taking a walk is one of the simplest, least expensive, physical, mental, and spiritual health improving activities that many of us can choose to do.

"Walk it off," somebody said, "when you're angry or upset."

Walk to think. Walk to cleanse your mind and strengthen your brain. Walk to dream. Walk and pray. Walk to catch a second wind.

Walk to burn some calories. Walking with children is fun. Walking to get a break from children is just as much fun.

Walk in love and you will attract God's blessings to yourself. It is automatic, such that when you love your neighbor as Jesus loves, showers of blessings are released to you when you least expect it. Therefore, if you want to experience God's awesome blessings, the best thing to do is to love unconditionally.

Who is your neighbor? Whomever is close to you at the moment.

Your ability to love will be perfected with practice. Negatives will be abolished from your life. Just do it!

MY PARENTS

"It is not enough to do your best; you must know what to do, and then do your best."

My mother, whose law enforcement father was killed during the Fidel Castro Revolution, immigrated to the United States from Cuba in the late 1940s. She met my father, who had moved from upstate New York to Manhattan, a migrant farm worker from Puerto Rico who was rejected from the U.S. Army draft due to a hearing impairment. They met while living in the same rooming house in New York City.

My mother worked in a sewing factory and my father worked in a grocery store. Dad was the only admirer that my grandmother approved of. They dated, and married after a year or so, then moved to Brighton Beach and had three children.

During the early years we had a lot of fun as a family, but by 1958, my parents had separated a few times and were on their way to a devastating divorce. Neither one was willing to change. I think parents need God in their lives in order to lead and endure.

LONELINESS

Loneliness is a feeling, and feelings pass. It is universal—a feeling that every human is bound to feel at some point... unless they've become a blood-sucking cling-on. LOL.

I'm sure you understand this, but the clinging can backfire, and they grow even lonelier because no one really likes a clingy needy human being. It's just uncomfortable. To me it's kind of how I feel about mosquitos. So, be social and funny and kind. Hang out, but don't *cling*.

How then can we handle loneliness? First, loneliness is yours to feel, and for a reason. Try to learn from it, but don't forget feelings do pass.

Ask yourself: *What am I doing or not doing? What can I change?* Socialize every time you get a good chance to. Sit with people. Invite others to do the simplest of things—a walk, a ride to wherever. Then enjoy people with all of their quirks and bad habits. After all, putting up with each other is a great skill.

Keep learning. Learn to like yourself. Pets and hobbies help, but most importantly, learn to like your own company. Be positive, friendly, and SMILE! 😊

DECLUTTERING

As a man thinks, so is he.

Here is the real to do list. Cleaning up is good for you, but it's not easy. Declutter or distance yourself from anything that adds no value or joy to your life.

Gently remove whatever persistently irritates, lies, is fake, disrespectful, ignores you, annoys you, is unkind or self-centered, takes you for granted, causes pain, or too often distracts your attention and drains your energy. In other words, distance yourself from unwanted drama.

Even if you can just put a little extra space or time between you and the clutter, that little bit of clean-up will add to your peace of mind.

Do all things out of love. And try to keep an open mind, because sometimes things change, so hold on to your power to modify if necessary.

You can be free to enjoy life much more like it was meant to be lived—undisturbedly peaceful whenever possible, occupied with the joy of freedom. I gave away ten nail polishes that I don't use today. It's that simple.

BEING PRESENT

Matthew 6:31-34: *Therefore do not be anxious, saying, 'What shall we eat?' or 'What shall we drink?' or 'What shall we wear?' For the Gentiles seek after all these things, and your heavenly Father knows that you need them all. But seek first the kingdom of God and his righteousness, and all these things will be added to you. Therefore, do not be anxious about tomorrow, for tomorrow will be anxious for itself. Sufficient for the day is its own trouble. (ESV)*

One day at a time, being right here, right now, fully present at this moment is the only real living there is. Being present helps us appreciate what we have and how blessed we are right now. Yesterday is gone; tomorrow has not yet arrived, and there is no certainty that it will, even though we have faith and hope for it to come. It is but an illusion. We cannot touch tomorrow except maybe with a prayer.

Don't go running in your thoughts to later on, tomorrow, or next week. Stay in today and enjoy it. Keep your focus and feelings on the tasks at hand. You will feel better after having done a good job at being present.

When you're at the gym, be at the gym, fully engaged in your workout. Turn off your phone if you dare, or leave it in the car. If you're eating, enjoy your food. If you're doing the dishes, feel the warmth of the water on your hands. Smell the suds. Focus fully on what you're doing.

Breathe deeply. Practice good posture, and just be. Bring your focus back to the task at hand whenever you're distracted. It's not easy but it's not perfection we are after. Just progress. Focus. Intent. The more you practice, the more you will be present. Just do it.

See, smell, taste, touch, hear. Perceive what is here and now and embrace it. Know that it is good. What we have now is enough.

Letting go of all else, just one moment, one step, one day at a time... take a minute to dwell on each task when accomplished.

Sometimes when I fly through my busy days, I can't even remember what I did, much less pat myself on the back for how hard I worked and how much I did. Being present is one way we can break up with stress.

FITNESS

Philippians 4:13: *I can do all things through Him who strengthens me. (ESV)*

I'm thankful for my body, which includes my brain. I am asked to take care of and develop whatever gifts I've been given. My body has always responded well to exercise and play. I noticed this when I was a child. I had a good body; it worked and was strong, but I could make it even stronger when I tried.

When I was a young child, I seemed to be sick quite a bit, then later in my teens I often had respiratory issues. At twenty, I developed wheezing and asthma. At twenty-three, I needed surgery to remove gallstones. I always liked exercising at the gym, either solo or in group classes. But I soon realized there was more to my health. There was the nutrition part that could make me sick in spite of my exercise and swimming.

I loved being active, being outdoors, walking, breathing... but there was more. And I am still learning. I am learning to believe in what I already know so that I'm not jumping from one diet trend to another. Good food has always been and will always be good food, and most of us know what's good by now.

I just need to do what I know is right most of the time, and be graceful with myself when I do the wrong thing... yet get back on track. Good people fail on a daily basis, but we get up and try again because we know that we are able to do better than this.

And oh yes, the best fitness tool for physical and mental health is *your smile!*

CARING ABOUT OTHERS
AS WE CARE ABOUT OURSELVES

Acts 20:35: Help the weak. It is more blessed to give than to receive.

I'm convinced that caring for others is the greatest teaching, aside from a personal relationship with God. When we care about others, we are not immune to life's pain and heartache, but in the end, the path is worse when we are too selfish.

Apparently, there are universal laws like "what you do returns to you" (cause and effect) that perpetuate the good or evil we choose for ourselves. Being self-absorbed is a tough problem because generally other people see it in us more than we can. It is sad but true. This is also why we need honest friends and self-reflection.

We all have choices to make, we all need to look, see, and check our thoughts and actions. Choosing not to doesn't prevent that law from causing the results to return to us—be they good or bad and on any level. Denial does not protect us. It ultimately makes us more vulnerable.

I suppose the best thing we can do is trace the origin or cause of the ripple that we so dislike... and change it. Turn it around. That is sometimes called repentance, one of the greatest gifts we've ever been offered. It is the only move that can change a pawn into a queen in real life.

I don't keep count, but I pay attention to being kind and resetting my attitude when I am wrong. This is a great blessing in terms of the victorious positive day by day evolution of my soul. Just care a little bit more every day. It adds up to peace and joy that I hadn't been able to imagine.

"Imagination is more powerful than intelligence."
—Albert Einstein

LIVE AND LEARN

What are you good at? I mean really, really good at? Things that random people compliment you about. Tasks that bring you joy when you look at what you've accomplished. What comes easily to you?

For me some form of creativity is usually involved. The things I want to do most feel like a form of play because I get so much joy out of doing them that it doesn't feel like work. Some are often easy because I've been doing them for so long that I can't even remember when I started. But for others, I have to study, learn, and intentionally practice. A lot. For example, I am not the most disciplined piano student, but the more I learn, the more I enjoy playing.

Time is life, so spending time both living and learning usually results in joy for me.

Life was meant to be lived—to be really lived and appreciated. Find and learn about your areas of strength and try to practice them with joy on a daily basis. Notice your weaknesses and work on those. But *live* and truly enjoy your strengths.

GRATITUDE

If I say just *one* thing—one little or big thing that I am truly thankful for each day—my life is positively changing, because the most influential words in my life are the ones I speak about myself.

Yes, it may hurt my feelings if someone speaks negative words about me, that's true. But fortunately, the words that I speak about myself have the most impact and strongest effect. What an amazing gift I can give myself. It's like auto-correct.

It's great to receive accolades and compliments for a job well done. But I will not depend upon other people to give me praise for my accomplishments. I actually must encourage myself in order to grow consistently and make steady progress in achieving my visions, dreams, and goals. I must replay them.

Today I am thankful for the revelation that when I practice gratitude even once a day, the rest of my life gets brighter and brighter.

Try it for a month... and I'm pretty sure you will never stop. Just jot down one thing each day in your calendar before bedtime and you will see. Smile!

NURTURERS AND WATERERS

There are people specifically placed in your life's path who will nurture you back to health, people who are capable and willing to care for you, folks who will feed and water your dreams. Much like the Good Samaritan.

Try very hard not to allow weeds to grow—people who are not capable of love—to crowd your life's space. The ones you have chosen to be in your inner circle must be healthy for your own growth, folks who help you thrive, and of course for whom you do the same. I like to keep my garden healthy.

It is not so very complicated or grandiose. It could simply be a smile, an encouraging word, a gift, a favor, a pat on the back, a caring phone call or text. Once in a while someone may choose to do something really great for you. The thing is that you will be wise to pay attention and to keep your own mind clear of clutter so you can discern and respond appropriately.

People get close to you for different reasons. It is wise if you can discern what the reason is, so that you too can nurture the good seeds and get the weeds out of your lovely precious path.

May you always blossom and be beautiful!

I LOVE WRITING

Writing draws my hidden memories to the surface much like a rollercoaster ride draws fear and excitement. Do I tell all the truth that I know? Do I have the courage and wherewithal? Do I expose my own sins or only the shortcomings of others? Do I stop hiding and being afraid to fully be me, or am I writing in order to stop hiding away my God-given gifts and testimony?

Do I think about why I did this or that? Or why he or she did it to me? Or do I simply write my memories according to Iris? "Let go and let God," my mother told me at least a hundred times.

I am already very popular as well as very not so popular, because some people love to hear truth and others hate it. "*But it is my truth*," I say to console myself.

First Corinthians 13:12 says, "Now, we only see in part like through a glass half dim. Then we will see clearly and face to face."

I love the promise of heaven. Heaven, the place where all things work out so well (well, not *work out* but are *made*), and so accurately that there are no more mistakes, tears, discomforts, insecurities, sins, diseases, or pain. Where nothing is missing and no one is needy or broken. Where everybody is healed and happy. What a promise! Can we even imagine this perfection? Can we dwell on heaven without discarding the beauty and great blessing of life here on earth in the present moment?

We aim. We aim to please, to do what is best, to fix and help to change and grow, yet we are all of us in the same boat... until that great day! Some know more, some less. The key is learning from everyone you meet.

For me, writing is a great way to remember deep painful occurrences that I have conveniently put away in my mind. Although some are disappointments in other people and others downright abuse, my questions remain: *Do I do unto others as they have done to me? Do I give myself more grace and confidentiality than what I am willing to give others? Or do I use one kind of writing to vent, see, and know more clearly, yet another to tell my story and share encouragement in a more joyful manner?*

You probably know what I'm thinking. I love writing, the good and the bad of it.

LAUGHTER

Funny songs, funny movies, friends that make us laugh, seeing the humor in life situations... cracking up, best of all belly laughs. These are good for your body, mind, and spirit. Your soul rejoices in laughter. I am very blessed and lucky to be surrounded by so much comedy.

Laughter is the best medicine. It has been studied and proven. So, if we really want to feel better and stop complaining so much, then let's search out ways to laugh every day, and to be funny. You can even use your computer and television to help you be happier and healthier... *Laugh! HA!*

I told my girlfriend she drew her eyebrows too high. She seemed surprised.

A woman went into a library and asked if they had any books about paranoia. The librarian said, "They're right behind you!"

DECLUTTER YOUR LIFE

We need to be clear, clean, and collected. I love an unobstructed view, the ability to see clearly. I learned this living by the ocean in Sea Gate Brooklyn. Clutter doesn't blind us, but it is a constant distraction. It's like visual noise pollution. And that's just on the surface. On a deeper level, clutter blocks our ability to think freely with its chaotic attack on our memory, unnecessarily blocking God out.

If memory is largely based on repeatedly putting things in their place, then it stands to reason that the chaos of having more things than can easily be managed will harm the memory process. I will be unclear as to where I put my keys simply because I didn't put them in a place just for my keys. The more things and the more times I practice this messiness, the harder my brain has to work just to get myself together so I can get out of the house on time.

When I declutter my home, I declutter my mind as well. All of a sudden my mind becomes clearer. I feel rested. It becomes easier to let go of unwanted negativity and toxic people. My discernment gets sharpened. This has become a great ritual. And I feel cooler and more collected, so I keep doing it.

TAKE A RISK

Somebody said:

☆take a risk

☆try something new

☆go ahead, trust your instincts again

☆you cannot fail, you can only learn

I thought, "Okay, I'll study the piano once again. I'll sing. I'll lead worship. The doors will open for the gifts that are surely His."

Then I said, "I'll dare to dream again. The fearless dreams, not the controlled kind. It shall not be reckless or endanger anyone but it shall be a blessing."

I told my good teacher who masters musical encouragement and artistic security that I wanted to study music. "Okay," he said and brought out a brand-new book for learning the basic skills of improvisation... Yikes!

At the first lesson I was as awkward as a fish out of water. But I practiced and applied my faith to the task at hand. I kept wondering, *I have such great hearing and rhythm, but where has it all gone?* I felt like a pure klutz.

Today... I have discovered that it was all hiding underneath those assignments and only reappeared to bless my heart after I worked more diligently at the piano. So now I know how those musicians get hooked on learning how to play. Thank you, God, for freedom, for courage, for music, and for good kind teachers.

Last night I went to a Jazz session at Holy Hound Tavern downtown (yes, the one with the rather loud college crowd). I arrived with a new mindset. I wanted to learn more about that magical music called *Jazz improvisation* because, I don't know why, but I believe Jazz should be married to worship.

So now when I lead worship, the drummer on the team says, "I hear that Jazz coming through."

Secretly, I smile.

Who could ask for more?

FAMILY

Enjoy your family forever. Today is my brother's birthday. He would have been sixty-eight. I suppose that in heaven there is no age but only eternity. If all that I believe is true, then my dream last year where my brother appeared happy and safe is telling me of the goodness of God—the goodness that not even a mother can comprehend.

I am happy that my brother is no longer suffering. He maxed out on suffering on earth. He never complained. He tried to take life and deal with it, in the only ways he knew.

Happy Birthday from earth to my brother, who not only brought me much joy and love here, but continues to exude love in the hereafter. Enjoy the music... and whatever you do, don't call me on the phone!

FITNESS

Being fit is something I have always valued highly and actually enjoyed. Yet things have gotten in my way so that if I want to recover my fitness after an injury, aging, sadness, busyness, or tiredness from working all day, ironically I sometimes have to work hard to even get started again.

This tells me that there is a battle going on, an invisible opposition not only to my getting to work out, but to my own happiness. This I cannot allow, so if I fall, I get up again.

Then I start all over, no matter what. My body starts saying, "Look, I need exercise, girl. Don't forget about me, because me is you!" So off I go with the plan to get going!

PHYSICAL HUNGER

Sometimes I'm just really thirsty, but I think I'm hungry until I drink lots of water.

Sometimes I'm really tired, but I think I'm hungry so I crave sugar instead of resting.

Still other times I am sluggish, but think I'm hungry until I take a nice walk or have a little exercise.

So maybe it's true that it's good to eat three balanced meals—tipping toward more protein and less empty carbs. Drink water, especially with lemon slices, and then just rest well. Exercise and have a mid-morning and mid-afternoon satisfying glass of water and a healthy fruit and cheese stick.

You mean it's really that simple?

Well, after searching a million diets, that what I've learned. LOL.

LIVING AND LEARNING
THAT YOU HAVE POWER

Some children learn that they have power at a very young age. Their parents and grandparents, aunts and uncles spoil them as much as possible (hopefully, without creating monsters).

Other children may grow up feeling unwanted or like a burden. They may learn to help or stay out of the way because their home environment can get pretty loud, chaotic, or even dangerous. These children learn vigilance, watching their words and actions. They may not be as trusting... or perhaps they become too trusting. There's really no figuring it out. But one thing is for sure. We were all born with innate *power!*

Some of us wield it like a scary superhero, while others quietly plan their actions (sometimes too carefully). But life was meant to be lived. Find your areas of strength and use them daily. Notice your weaknesses and work on those. But *live!*

BULLIES

I stay far away from bullies. Bullies look gigantic, and they might be. But on the inside, they can be small, sad, and very insecure people.

The bullies I have encountered were so weak on the inside that they actually wanted to be like me. They often despise themselves; they can't stand the idea that someone can be different and strong, so they try to tear you down... to "cut you down to size." They leave you out and make sure you feel guilty.

It can be because they perceive their own weakness when they are around people like you. Maybe you get higher grades. Maybe you have self-control that is foreign to them. You might be better at anything at all, and that somehow is interpreted as "I'm just not good enough." They can't compliment you for your God-given gifts.

Bullies are very insecure people. They can be loud, controlling, divisive, violent, quiet, or cunning... the outside doesn't really matter that much. Just take care of yourself and get away from them. Any distance is better than none.

TRUTH

Somebody said, "The truth hurts." But I think that lies hurt even more, and for a longer period of time. Lies are very damaging.

Lies keep us coming back for the truth. I am like this to an extreme level. I grew up having to find out what was true and what was right much of the time. I only survived by continuously seeking truth.

If someone has a lot to hide, and is not honest and open, forthright and authentic, I doubt they can be a good friend. So, I should not spend so much time figuring them out. I should not waste time and energy wondering and asking questions. If they wanted to tell me the truth, they just would.

Spend time living your own truth, doing what you know to be the right thing to do this day. That's enough. This is the day of salvation. Not yesterday, and not tomorrow.

HAVING A PITY PARTY

"Self-pity in its early stages is as snug as a feather mattress. Only when it hardens does it become uncomfortable."

—Maya Angelou, *Gather Together in My Name*

One day a very long time ago, I was feeling blue, like Eeyore. I started to recount all the terrible things that had happened to me in recent days... be they relational, physical, work-related, or parental. In my journal I wrote "I'm having a pity party."

This wisdom from Maya Angelou explains something important. Being self-centered is almost never a good thing, so if you really must feel sorry for yourself, for a minute or a day, make it very short. For when it hardens, pity becomes incredibly uncomfortable.

"Parties weren't meant to last!" —*Prince*

MONEY

"Saving" means paying yourself first.

"For a rainy day" means for the unexpected.

Save your change, your small bills and big bills. Save money in a piggy bank. In a box. In a nicely colored envelope tucked into a good book about money. In a glass jar.

Save for new purchases and fun adventures.

Learn to like having money. "Do not despise small beginnings." Start with a penny if you must, and add an extra penny each day. Or make it two pennies on the second day and then three on and on. Keep multiplying.

Money can buy some happiness, but the lack thereof can surely cause a lot of unnecessary stress, strife, and turmoil. Trust me, I came from a family of spenders, living only for the moment.

Somebody coached that when you get your first job, don't cash the first seven checks. Then you can decide what's best after your discipline makes you smile big and wide, when you see how much you've accumulated.

My sister was the biggest saver in my family. From the time we were small, she treasured her big pink piggy bank. Saving is financial security.

It's "the love of money" (turning it into an idol) that is the "root of all evil."

Oh yeah, and remember that "money doesn't grow on trees." You work hard for it, so ask yourself this before you buy anything: *Can I afford this? Will it be a treasure? Does it bring me joy?* Ask yourself: *How can I make my money grow and work for me, instead of me always working for it?*

I really believe that generosity is one great way to make money grow. Sharing and not holding too tightly to your money is a miracle that multiplies your blessings.

ENVY

Envy lives on dangerous ground, close to jealousy. But envy is dangerous to our bodies and souls when it becomes a habitual practice. Everyone probably thinks, *Oh, wouldn't it be great to have this or that?* Something that someone else has, whether it be a new car, job, or relationship that shines. But all that glitters is not gold. To dwell on this kind of thought makes one actually feel sick on the inside, so much so that physiologically, one may be inclined to react when the object of envy is seen or remembered.

Some people go as far as wanting to separate a couple, a friendship, or a person from their position at work because they cannot stand this feeling of envy that takes them over. We must learn to master our emotions.

We cannot control other people, but we can dismiss our own negative thoughts, then say a quick prayer and replace them with positive thankfulness for all the blessings we do have.

REST

When we get bombarded and are trying really hard to deal with things—like work, play, bills, income, friends, family, devotions, prayers, deaths, illness— we must find chunks of recovery time to do what heals and refreshes us.

Take a barefoot walk in the yard, find a book to read, work a puzzle, sing a song, write in a journal.

We need our time and space... time to just be with our Creator, the one who knows all things and on whom we can rely. Rest and be revived.

NATURE

A walk in the woods in spring or fall... majestic mountains... birds on the ledge of the deck in the yard... working in the garden... waterfalls... oceans... digging in the soil and planting seeds, resurrecting dying plants... these are all things I have enjoyed.

Snow, rain, sunshine, a warm breeze in winter, or a cool breeze in summer... these are awesome things to enjoy.

Animals at the zoo, on a safari, pets at home... how blessed we are to experience the natural world around us.

To me, best of all is a week or two by the sea. What a gift!

WHAT IS DIFFERENT
ABOUT YOU?

1 Peter 2:9: But you are a chosen generation, a royal priesthood, a holy nation, His own special people, that you may proclaim the praises of Him who called you out of darkness into His marvelous light. (NKJV)

What is that smile and laughter about? Why are you so joyful? It makes you stand out. A light shining in the darkness. Kindness and sincerity are rare.

What is that difference I see in you? People wonder. The way you move through the world... the tender words you speak... the way you cry. I just want to know what is that difference that I see in you? What is all your hope about?

It might be just what I need.

GEEZ, I THOUGHT
I COULD FIX IT

Sometimes relationships break down. Sometimes they never get started, but we think they do. A vital key to good relationships of any kind is honesty. It's a great idea to solely deal with honest people, especially in your inner circle. The problem is that people who lie are easy to meet. And sometimes you can't detect the lies, especially if the people are busy lying to even themselves or putting on a front.

But time will tell you. Red flags will show up. Try hard not to ignore them. Your inner witness will be disturbed by things a liar says or does. It's the incongruencies, the little things that make you say *"What??"*

Pay attention. Step back a little, because you probably can't fix this. Most likely you wouldn't drive a broken car that needs repairs for very long… it's the same with relationships.

REAL FRIENDS

It has never been easy to know who your *real* friends are, and in these days of social media, people are much more distant, yet we talk to each other. This can be a great thing, catching up with people we grew up with or people we see at the local coffee shop, at work, church, gym, or at a pub.

We now have a larger number of "friends," or acquaintances, so to speak. But this makes knowing who our real true friends are even more challenging and important!

Some ways to know our real friends is that they genuinely care about us. They try to communicate with us when they have time because they nurture and grow friendship *with* us. In other words, they do at least half the work... because true friendship takes nurturing, like a lovely garden.

You are there for each other if needed. This is important because people who live extremely far away cannot take a walk with you, or go shopping, or come to visit you, or drop off soup when you feel under the weather. Those are things a friend does joyfully and willingly. Always be a friend so that you will always have a friend. 😊

SMILES

When you're sad, it's good to cry, but always smile afterward.

Smiling brings more company. It attracts people that are glad to be alive. So, after you cry it out, remember to bring on that award-winning smile of yours.

It takes less energy to smile than it does to frown. And frowns bring people down. Sometimes I just look in the mirror for a while and rehearse my smiles. Don't worry, be happy.

When I was thirteen, I really wanted dimples. They looked so cute on smiling friends. But I wasn't born with dimples so I decided that I could somehow create dimples on my cheeks. I would practice smiling all kinds of smiles for hours in the mirror. I tried to perfect the ones that created any semblance of cutie-pie dimples. LOL.

The thing is... sadness is okay. After all, it's a human response to disappointment or hurt. But sadness sometimes wants to park in your private space forever. Refuse to allow it to hang out too long. A ten-minute pity party is more than enough.

One time I remember envisioning and feeling this dark cloud-type depression trying to attach itself to me. It even had tentacles like an octopus. I denied it any entrance. It was a battle, but I did not give in. Sometimes we must fight and win emotional or spiritual battles. We can't give in.

Keep smiling! You look beautiful when you smile. And the world smiles with you. 😊

YOU'RE GOING TO NEED MONEY

1 Timothy 6:10: For the love of money is a root of all kinds of evil. Some people, eager for money, have wandered from the faith and pierced themselves with many griefs. (NIV)

When I was a little girl, I was very observant. I came from a family that was half Cuban and half Puerto Rican. One day as I was pondering a vision (as children often do) and trying to make sense out of life, I asked myself a question. *Which side of my family do I like most?* Like all children do, I only considered the things I had seen and heard in my home. I determined the answer very gently as follows.

Both sides are so kind and generous to me. They all love to get together often and celebrate. Really a rich beautiful heritage, now that I look back.

But then I had to decide which side I liked best and why. Well there's one side that loves flaunting clothing and jewelry and prosperity. You know, "showing off." The other side was way more natural and down to earth, I thought. So that was my favorite, but I loved them all. Natural just seems easier to me.

Money is a tricky thing to get, to pay, to save, to give, to share, and to earn, yet it is a necessity. A vital thing about money is that it can be tempting to change who you inherently are and value in exchange for a promised pile of money. I decided early on that I couldn't do that!

Even so, I've had expensive taste ever since I was old enough to know about value. My family was hard working but never financially rich. And the one rich grand-uncle was a criminal.

I was a learner. And I learned to work hard at a job that I enjoy. I learned that your gifts will make a way for you, and that God will always provide for His own children.

So, save up for a rainy day. Keep the value of money in a realistic balance because you can't take it with you, and you don't want to gain the whole world only to lose your soul, baby.

GETTING INVOLVED

No matter who you are, where you are, or how much time you have, there are many great opportunities for you to get involved and be part of the solution.

Whatever issue makes you really mad is probably an indication of where you could begin to research good volunteer opportunities.

Pray about it. Think about it. What do people appreciate most about you or say that you're really good at? Step out in faith.

Find that place and then donate, volunteer, serve.

Evil reigns when good people do *nothing*.

THE PAIN OF LIFE

Pain is certainly real.

Sometimes we are hurt by others, and sometimes we fall.

Some people are certainly mean-spirited or callous. Sometimes we are. But the important thing to remember is that we are also resilient.

We heal. We are "the healed, not the perfect." So never give up believing that you can and will be better, because you can and will feel better.

Just believe!

HEALTH

3 John 1:2: Beloved, I pray that you may prosper in every way and [that your body] may keep well, even as [I know] your soul keeps well and prospers.

I like to agree with the Word, in word and in deed, as much as possible. Oftentimes I have failed at this, but I try and try again because there is a blessing in it.

Good health allows us to do so many things that we often take for granted but that we should be thankful for many times a day because health is easy to lose.

When we lose our good health, we usually suffer. Now, that's not all bad because we can also be blessed in suffering, yet I believe it is His will that we prosper and be in good health even as our souls prosper.

Studies show us that the state of our mind, will, and emotions dictates the quality of our physical health. So whatever state we are in, we can get healthier every day, one way or another. Find a way.

Here's to your health!

CARING FOR YOUR SELF

We are grownups now, which means we must continue to grow and mature. A lot of people take care of children, the elderly, the disabled, and even their pets. But when we are able adults, it is also our precious privilege and blessed responsibility to take care of ourselves—our own physical, spiritual, and emotional well-being... our own rest, recreation, work, play, fitness, and social life.

Of course, there may be some really kind souls who inspire, motivate, or even help us to do this... but this is a great freedom and honor, and if done well, our future selves will very graciously thank us.

INTENSE WORKDAYS

Colossians 3:23: *Work willingly at whatever you do, as though you were working for the Lord rather than for people. (NLT)*

Relax to get rid of the tension, both in your head and in your body.

I'll eat clean food for dinner, drink plenty of water, and workout. I'll watch comedies and sports in order to avoid political news. I'll have some fruit and be thankful. I will listen to inspiring music while I'm on the treadmill because it was a very intense day in court. Some people got what they wanted, and others got what was coming to them. Some men were scared, others crying. The staff was doing their best to keep things pleasant, but the stress was inevitable. The tension was tangible.

My answer is always retreat and prayer, because tomorrow is another day... and we must be ready to go again.

ACKNOWLEDGMENTS

I would like to thank all of the people who inspired and encouraged me to write this book. Thank you for your patience and tenacity.

Thanks to my mother who always told me she wanted to write a book about her life, but didn't get to.

Thanks to Ernie Zimmerman, a family man, a relentless encourager, Vietnam veteran, and fellow writer and NYPD Brooklynite.

Thank you to my family for their kind, loving actions toward me. They mean the world to me.

ABOUT THE AUTHOR

An adventurous child of God, IRIS FERBER quit high school due to family financial needs. Nevertheless, Iris loved learning, libraries, and play. She has a relentless desire to seek truth. She is passionate about music, singing, and most of all, God and people.

Iris is a seasoned language interpreter who grew up in Brighton Beach, Brooklyn, New York, in a loving, complicated, Spanish-speaking family. She now lives in central Pennsylvania, and has three adult children and seven grandchildren.

38485949R00092